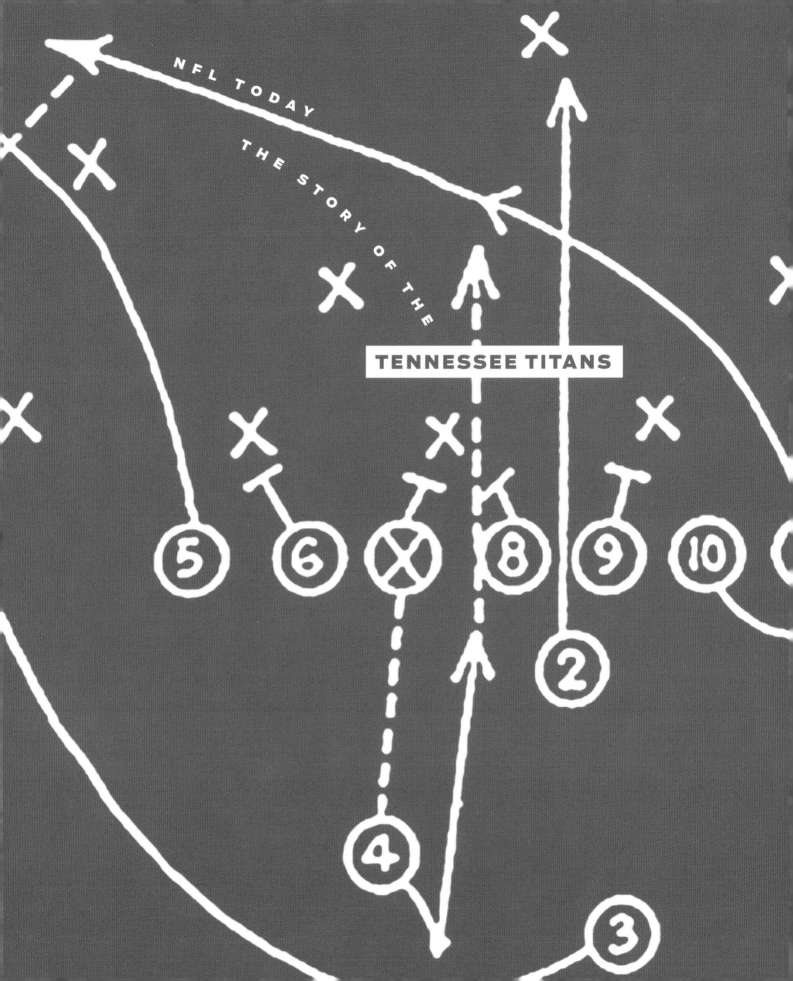

NFL TODAY

THE STORY OF THE

TENNESSEE TITANS

THE STORY OF THE TENNESSEE TITANS

CREATIVE EDUCATION

PUBLISHED BY CREATIVE EDUCATION
P.O. BOX 227, MANKATO, MINNESOTA 56002
CREATIVE EDUCATION IS AN IMPRINT OF THE CREATIVE COMPANY
WWW.THECREATIVECOMPANY.US

DESIGN AND PRODUCTION BY BLUE DESIGN
ART DIRECTION BY RITA MARSHALL
PRINTED IN THE UNITED STATES OF AMERICA

PHOTOGRAPHS BY AP IMAGES (ASSOCIATED PRESS),
CORBIS (BETTMANN), GETTY IMAGES (BRIAN BAHR,
SCOTT BOEHM, GARY BOGDON/SPORTS ILLUSTRATED,
FREDERICK BREEDON, JONATHAN DANIEL, JONATHAN
DANIEL/ALLSPORT, JEROME DAVIS/NFL, TONY DUFFY/
ALLSPORT, STEPHEN DUNN, CHAD EHLERS, FOCUS
ON SPORT, GEORGE GOJKOVICH, SAM GREENWOOD,
GRANT HALVERSON, PAUL JASIENSKI, ALLEN KEE/
NFL, NEIL LEIFER/SPORTS ILLUSTRATED, ANDY LYONS,
AL MESSERSCHMIDT/NFL, JOSEPH PATRONITE, DOUG
PENSINGER, MARK PERLSTEIN/TIME & LIFE PICTURES,
PAUL SPINELLI, MATTHEW STOCKMAN, LOU WITT/NFL,
MICHAEL ZAGARIS)

LIBRARY OF CONGRESS CATALOGING-IN-PUBLICATION DATA
GILBERT, SARA.
THE STORY OF THE TENNESSEE TITANS / SARA GILBERT.
P. CM. — (NFL TODAY)
INCLUDES INDEX.
SUMMARY: THE HISTORY OF THE NATIONAL FOOTBALL LEAGUE'S
TENNESSEE TITANS, SURVEYING THE FRANCHISE'S BIGGEST
STARS AND MOST MEMORABLE MOMENTS FROM ITS INAUGURAL
SEASON IN 1960 TO TODAY.
ISBN 978-1-60818-322-7
1. TENNESSEE TITANS (FOOTBALL TEAM)—HISTORY—JUVENILE
LITERATURE. I. TITLE.

GV956.T45G55 2013
796.332'640976855—DC23   2012033820

FIRST EDITION
9 8 7 6 5 4 3 2 1

COVER: QUARTERBACK JAKE LOCKER
PAGE 2: RUNNING BACK LENDALE WHITE
PAGES 4–5: 2007 TENNESSEE TITANS
PAGE 6: WIDE RECEIVER DARIUS REYNAUD

TABLE OF CONTENTS

DOWNTOWN NASHVILLE, TENNESSEE, OVERLOOKS THE CUMBERLAND RIVER

A Brilliant Beginning

Before Nashville, Tennessee, officially became a city in 1806, it was the site of an early American Indian culture, a favored hunting area, and an important river port and railroad hub for settlers traveling west from North Carolina. It later became the capital of Tennessee, the birthplace of country music, and the center of the United States Civil Rights Movement in the 1950s and '60s. Later still, Nashville became a popular destination for fans of auto racing, minor league baseball, and other sports.

Not until 1998, however, did the Southern city become known for its own football team. That year, the National Football League (NFL) moved the Houston Oilers franchise and its 40-year history northeast to Nashville, the "Athens of the South," where it adopted a name inspired by Greek mythology and became known as the Tennessee Titans.

The Titans franchise started on the dusty plains of Texas in 1959, when a wealthy oil businessman named K. S. "Bud" Adams joined forces with seven other millionaires who wanted to own professional football teams. Together, they formed a new league called

QUARTERBACK GEORGE BLANDA PLAYED PRO FOOTBALL FOR AN ASTOUNDING 26 SEASONS

Bud Adams

TEAM OWNER / OILERS/TITANS SEASONS: 1960—PRESENT

From the Oilers' beginnings in Houston to the Titans' Tennessee home today, K. S. "Bud" Adams Jr. has been in the owner's seat, guiding his franchise every step of the way. After Adams started the ADA Oil Company in 1946, the wealthy Texas businessman sponsored amateur teams in basketball and softball and held ownership stakes in professional basketball, baseball, and boxing. In 1959, Adams wanted to join the NFL with a team in Houston, but the league turned him down. So he helped create the AFL, which rivaled the NFL for a decade before it was absorbed by the NFL in 1970. Adams began searching for a new stadium for the Oilers as early as 1987, when he publicly talked to Jacksonville, Florida, about a possible relocation. Eight years later, Nashville, Tennessee, agreed to build a stadium for the team, and Adams announced that the Oilers would move for the 1997 season. Although he spent big bucks on his Titans, Adams also believed in giving back to the community. By 2012, local Tennessee charities had received approximately $20 million as a result of Adams's charitable work.

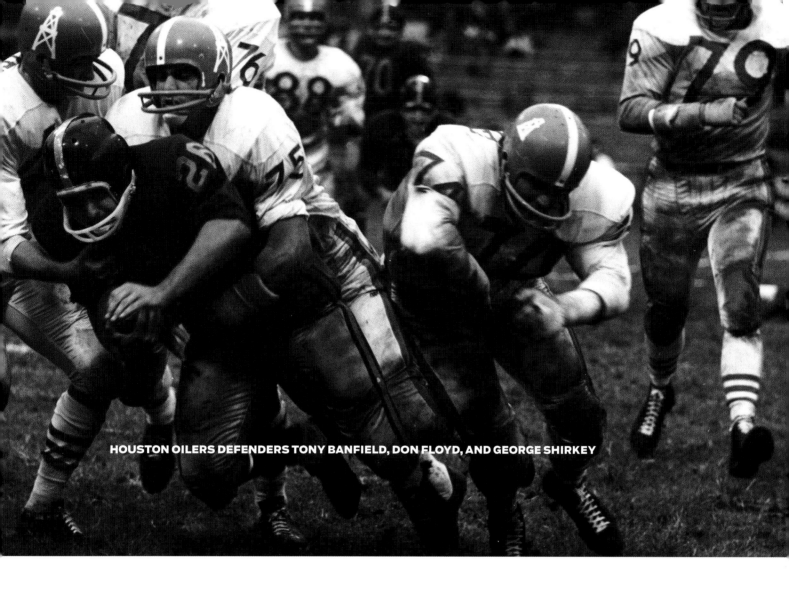

HOUSTON OILERS DEFENDERS TONY BANFIELD, DON FLOYD, AND GEORGE SHIRKEY

the American Football League (AFL), and Adams named his team the Oilers, after the natural resource so plentiful in Texas.

At first, most AFL players were either old, former NFL players or undrafted college players. But Oilers head coach Lou Rymkus was able to sign running back Billy Cannon, who had just won the Heisman Trophy as the best player in college football, by doubling the $50,000-a-year contract the Los Angeles Rams had offered to Cannon. The NFL challenged the contract in court, and the Oilers won, which boosted the AFL's credibility as a professional league.

The Oilers' first roster also featured quarterback George Blanda. While many football observers thought the veteran was washed up, Blanda proved his worth by throwing 24 touchdown passes in the Oilers' first season, mostly to receivers Charley Hennigan and Bill Groman. Blanda also occasionally doubled as the team's kicker, making 15 field goals and 46 points after touchdowns. Joining Cannon and Blanda in Houston's backfield was running back Charley Tolar, who was nicknamed the "Human Bowling Ball." At just 5-foot-6, Tolar had a knack for charging underneath taller defenders.

"nicknamed the 'Human Bowling Ball.'"

ON RUNNING BACK CHARLEY TOLAR

In their debut season, the Oilers went 10–4 and won the AFL's Eastern Division championship. They then went on to play the Los Angeles Chargers in the AFL Championship Game. Houston hosted 32,000 fans for the game at Jeppesen Stadium, a renovated high school field that the Oilers called home. After Los Angeles grabbed an early lead with two field goals, Blanda and the Oilers were up 10–9 at halftime. The veteran quarterback then tossed a swing pass to Cannon for a fourth-quarter score, and the Oilers won, 24–16. Later, Blanda would look back on the 1960 Oilers and boast, "That first year, the Houston Oilers or the Los Angeles Chargers could have beaten the NFL champion [Philadelphia Eagles] in a Super Bowl."

Midway through the following season, Wally Lemm took over as coach. Under Lemm, the Oilers averaged 41 points a game over their last 9 games. Cannon led the charge with an AFL-best 948 rushing yards and 15 touchdowns. The Oilers finished the season with a 10–3–1 record and another trip to the league title game, where they met the Chargers again. The second AFL Championship Game was heavy on defense, and the Oilers won 10–3 for their second title. Strong and speedy Oilers defensive end Don Floyd frustrated the Chargers, and an interception by Oilers defensive back Julian Spence clinched the win. "I feel like someone who inherited a million dollars in tarnished silverware," said Coach Lemm. "All I did was polish it."

Oilers fans were hoping for a "three-peat" in 1962 when the team again won the Eastern Division and faced another Texas team, the Dallas Texans, for the league championship. The Oilers tied the game in the fourth quarter when Tolar dove into the end zone for a one-yard score, and the game went into the first of two overtimes. In the end, though, Houston came up short, losing 20–17. That loss signaled the start of a disappointing stretch for the Oilers and their fans. Age and injury began to bog down the team, and Houston finished the next four seasons with losing records.

The Oilers finally got back above .500 in 1967 after adding such terrific players as safety Ken Houston, linebacker George Webster, and 6-foot-9 defensive tackle Ernie Ladd. Houston's power shifted to the defensive side of the ball, and the team allowed opponents to score an average of only 14 points per game on the season—the lowest in the league. The Oilers won their division with a 9–4–1 record but were unable to capture the AFL title, losing to the Oakland Raiders in the championship game.

Double-Overtime in Texas

Nearly 38,000 fans packed Houston's Jeppesen Stadium in December 1962 to watch a championship battle between the AFL's two Texas teams, the Houston Oilers and the Dallas Texans. For the Texans, the bout would be their last game representing Dallas. They were planning on moving to Kansas City, Missouri, where they would become the Chiefs. The Oilers, meanwhile, were hoping to claim their third straight AFL championship. At halftime, the Texans led 17–0, but the Oilers staged a comeback—which included a George Blanda touchdown pass and field goal, followed by a touchdown run by running back Charley Tolar—to tie the game with less than six minutes on the clock. The Oilers had a chance at a game-winning field goal in the last seconds of regulation, but the Texans blocked it, sending the game into overtime. With no score after 15 minutes, the teams headed into a second overtime. This time, the Texans drove into field-goal range and ended the game with a 25-yard kick. The 20–17 Dallas win came after 78 minutes of play, making it one of the longest games in professional football history.

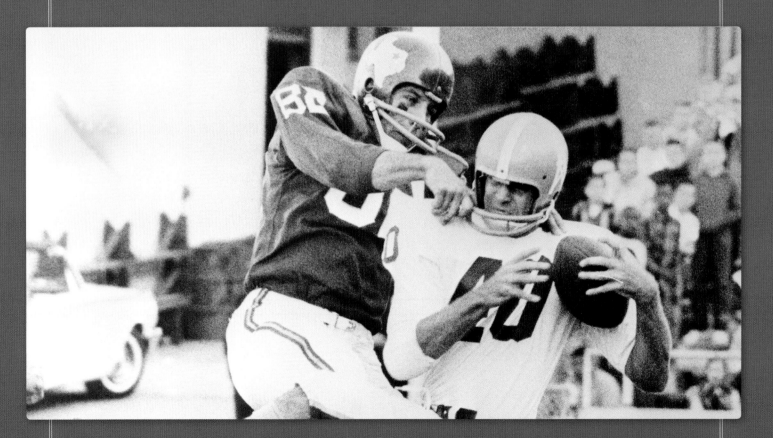

THE TEXANS SHOWED PERSEVERANCE IN SNAGGING THE CHAMPIONSHIP WIN

Defensive
end Elvin
Bethea, who
displayed a
frightening
combination of quickness,
power, and durability, joined
the Oilers in 1968. During his
16 seasons in Houston, he
played in a franchise-record
210 games and gave his all
in each one. Bethea's college
coach, Hornsby Howell,
later explained that Bethea
"was the kind of athlete who
worked hard even when
nobody was watching." But
despite strong performances
by Blanda, Houston, and
Bethea—all eventual Hall-of-
Famers—the Oilers couldn't
muster another winning
campaign in the 1960s.

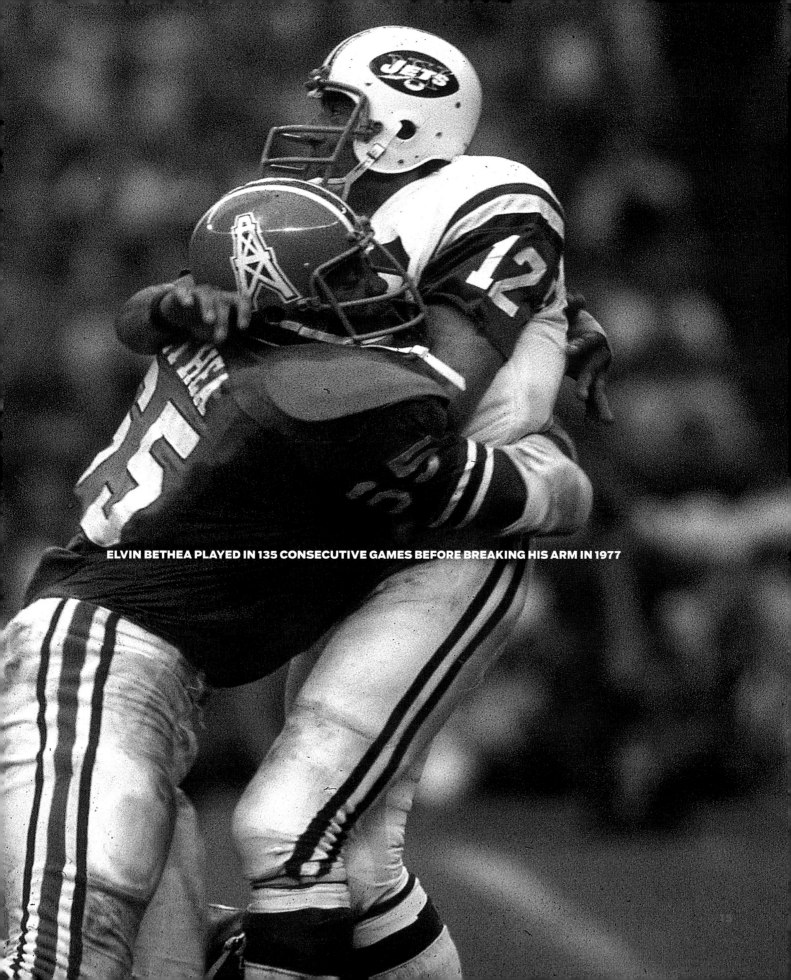

ELVIN BETHEA PLAYED IN 135 CONSECUTIVE GAMES BEFORE BREAKING HIS ARM IN 1977

Earl Campbell

RUNNING BACK / OILERS SEASONS: 1978–84 / HEIGHT: 5-FOOT-11 / WEIGHT: 232 POUNDS

Nicknamed the "Tyler Rose" (after his hometown of Tyler, Texas), Earl Campbell burst onto the professional football scene in 1978. The former Heisman Trophy winner was named both Offensive Rookie of the Year and the NFL's Most Valuable Player (MVP) after his debut season. Although Campbell was soft-spoken, there was nothing quiet about his playing style. He possessed great speed, incredible strength, and a powerful stiff arm, and he used them all to evade—or, more often, to barrel through—opposing defenders. His powerful thighs made him incredibly difficult to topple; defensive players usually had to gang-tackle him to bring him down. Despite the pounding his body took, he played in nearly every game, missing only 6 games out of 115 in Houston because of injury. During the 1980 season, Campbell rushed for more than 200 yards in 4 different games. In comparing Campbell with University of Oklahoma running back Billy Sims, who won the Heisman Trophy the year after Campbell did, Oklahoma Sooners coach Barry Switzer once said, "Earl Campbell is the greatest player that ever suited up. Billy Sims is human. Campbell isn't."

Feeling the Love

Before a *Monday Night Football* game on November 20, 1978, the Oilers handed out blue and white pompoms to 70,000 fans at the game. The hope was that the festive poms would help build on the spirit that had been growing in Houston since the season started. They did even more than that. Those pompoms started a fan movement that became known as "Luv Ya Blue." Fans began showing up at games with "Luv Ya Blue" painted on signs and on their cheeks. They held pep rallies. Win or lose, they pulled out all the stops to support their team. After the Oilers lost to the Pittsburgh Steelers in the 1978 playoffs, a local songwriter penned lyrics to a song named, predictably, "Luv Ya Blue." That song became the team's anthem and was played before the start of every home game in 1979. "The display of 'Luv Ya Blue' was a chance for people of all races and backgrounds to come together as a city," star running back Earl Campbell said. "More than that, it was a feeling that the players and fans shared without even talking."

HOUSTONIANS DISPLAYED PRIDE IN THEIR LOCAL TEAM IN THE LATE 1970s

Bum to the Rescue

After the AFL and NFL merged in 1970, the Oilers continued to struggle. Dan Pastorini, a tough quarterback known for his willingness to play through pain and injury, joined Houston as the team's first pick in the 1971 NFL Draft. But playing behind a weak offensive line, Pastorini was sacked often and rendered ineffective. In both 1972 and 1973, the Oilers finished an embarrassing 1–13.

The Oilers promoted defensive coordinator O. A. "Bum" Phillips to head coach in 1975, ushering in an era of increased fan support for the team. Phillips, who looked like the stereotypical Texan in his ten-gallon hat, snakeskin boots, and Western shirts, assembled a bruising defense that included Bethea and linebackers Gregg Bingham and Robert Brazile. Phillips used a "3-4" defense, with three linemen up front and four linebackers behind them—a

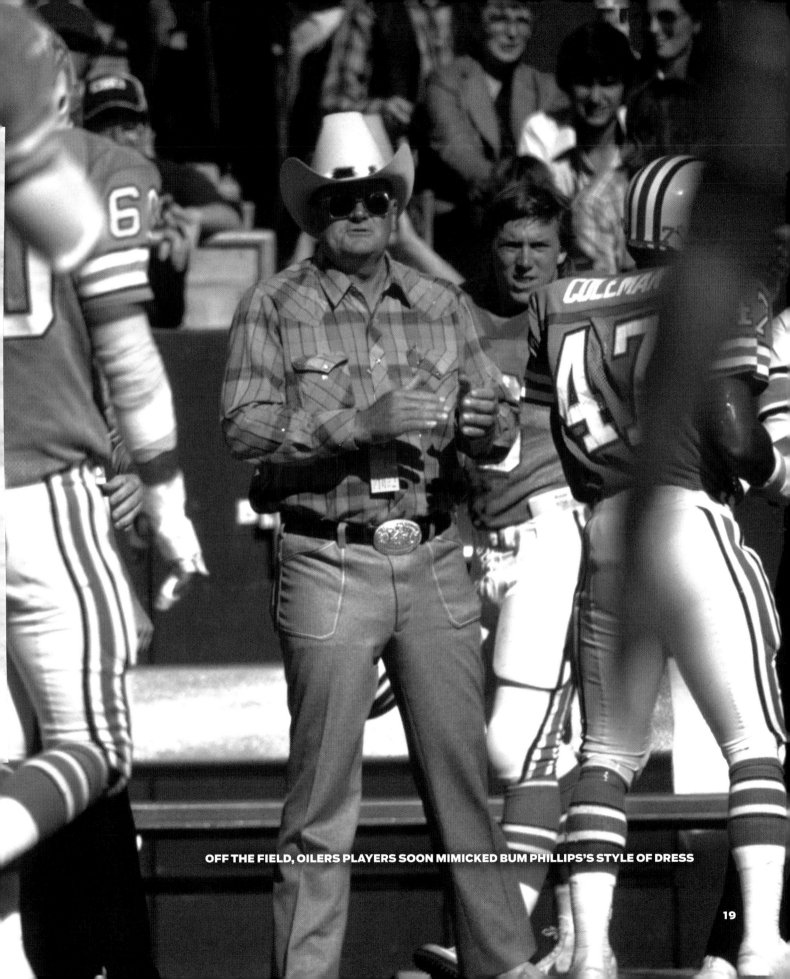

OFF THE FIELD, OILERS PLAYERS SOON MIMICKED BUM PHILLIPS'S STYLE OF DRESS

Warren Moon

QUARTERBACK / OILERS SEASONS: 1984–93 / HEIGHT: 6-FOOT-3 / WEIGHT: 218 POUNDS

Warren Moon was not drafted by an NFL team after finishing his college career. Undaunted, he refused to give up his dream of being a professional football quarterback. For six years, Moon played for the Edmonton Eskimos in the Canadian Football League, where the quarterback refined his skills and led his team to five Grey Cup titles as league champion. Moon finally made his way to the NFL when he joined the Oilers in 1984. Initially, he struggled with accuracy; during his first three seasons in the NFL, Moon threw for 40 touchdowns and 59 interceptions. Then, in 1986, the team implemented the "run-and-shoot" offense, which showcased Moon's rocket arm and quick feet. Oilers head coach Jack Pardee once said of Moon, "he's got the height, he's got a good arm, and he studies football—he's everything we're looking for in a quarterback." Known for throwing picture-perfect spirals, Moon became the face of the franchise, leading his team to the playoffs in each of his last seven years with the Oilers. In 2006, Moon became the first African American quarterback elected to the Pro Football Hall of Fame.

"He was even more exciting in practice."

BUM PHILLIPS ON BILLY
"WHITE SHOES" JOHNSON

formation that was effective at stopping the run. This defensive package, adopted from the University of Oklahoma, was just starting to spread to professional football.

On offense, Pastorini had two capable passing targets: receivers Ken Burrough and Billy "White Shoes" Johnson, who had joined the Oilers in 1971 and 1974 respectively. Known for his bright-white shoes and goofy end zone dances, Johnson would tie an NFL record in 1975 by returning four kicks for touchdowns. Although he stood just 5-foot-9, Johnson had a knack for darting away from his much larger opponents. "He was even more exciting in practice," Phillips said later. "We didn't have anyone who could tackle him."

Although the Oilers missed the playoffs in 1975, they went a solid 10–4 and had fans flocking to the Houston Astrodome (which had opened in 1965) and even creating special cheers and a theme song about the players and their Columbia blue uniforms. The Oilers were hit hard by injuries and went just 5–9 and 8–6 the next two seasons, but Houston emerged as a powerhouse in 1978. That year, the Oilers identified Earl Campbell, a 230-pound running back, as the best player available in the NFL Draft. Unfortunately, the Oilers were scheduled to pick 17th in the draft. Phillips negotiated with the Tampa Bay Buccaneers, offering them three draft picks, a third-round choice the following year, and Oilers tight end Jimmie Giles in exchange for the bruising running back known as the "Tyler Rose." A nationally televised *Monday Night Football* game against the Miami Dolphins that season let the Oilers showcase their new star, as Campbell rushed over and through defenders for 199 yards and 4 touchdowns. Fans began to call the Oilers the "Earlers."

With a 10–6 record, the Oilers finally reached the playoffs in 1978. They eked out a win over the Dolphins and then sailed past the New England Patriots, setting up a showdown with the Steelers in

The Run-and-Shoot

The "run-and-shoot" offense originated in the 1970s, but the pass-heavy strategy did not make its way into professional football playbooks until the 1980s. Oilers quarterbacks coach June Jones began using some of the run-and-shoot's concepts in 1987. When Jack Pardee took over as head coach in 1990, the Oilers went to a full-time run-and-shoot offense, in which quarterback Warren Moon would roll toward the sidelines and fire passes to receivers racing across or down the field. From 1990 to 1992, the Oilers led the NFL in passing yards, averaging 4,485 per season. However, with only one running back, four wide receivers, and no tight ends on the field, the strategy earned a reputation for being risky. Without a tight end or second running back to help the offensive line, the quarterback often was left vulnerable to blitzing defenders. By 1994, the Oilers had moved away from the run-and-shoot, and opposing defenders rejoiced. "Tell the owner thank you and tell the front office thank you," said Pittsburgh Steelers cornerback Rod Woodson. "I think defenses all over the league are going to be very relieved."

WARREN MOON BECAME THE OILERS' MOST DEPENDABLE RUN-AND-SHOOT PASSER

WIDE RECEIVER AND TIGHT END ERNEST GIVINS PRODUCED STEADY YARDAGE

Pittsburgh for the American Football Conference (AFC) championship. Playing on an icy field and facing Pittsburgh's famous "Steel Curtain" defense, the Oilers committed nine turnovers and lost, 34–5. Afterwards, the Oilers returned to the Astrodome, where about 50,000 vocal fans were waiting to show their support. "This is the beginning of 1979 for us," said receiver Mike Barber.

In 1979, the Oilers suffered another loss, this time 27–13, to Pittsburgh in a rematch for the AFC championship. The next year, the Oakland Raiders bounced Houston from the playoffs in the first round. Frustrated by the continued playoff failures, Bud Adams then fired Phillips as head coach.

By the early 1980s, most of the Oilers' stars had retired or moved on to other teams; Campbell, the brightest star, would be traded to the New Orleans Saints in 1984 for a first-round draft pick. Houston lacked solid leadership during those years and went through several coaches. The Oilers became known as one of the worst teams in the NFL, wrapping up their 1983 season at just 2–14.

Houston's decline began to turn around with the 1984 acquisition of quarterback Warren Moon, a

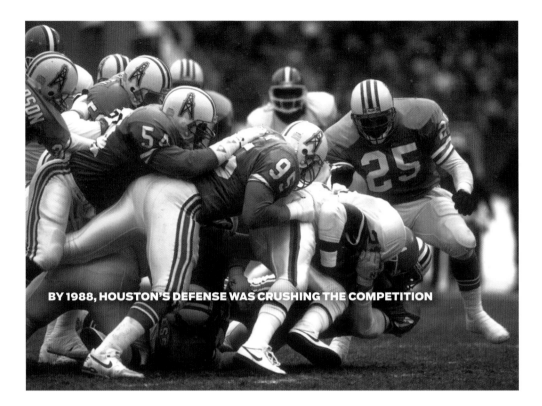

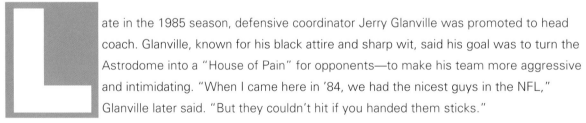
BY 1988, HOUSTON'S DEFENSE WAS CRUSHING THE COMPETITION

former Canadian Football League standout. After joining the Oilers, Moon began firing passes to the talented receiving trio of Drew Hill, Ernest Givins, and Haywood Jeffires. He completed his first NFL season with 3,338 passing yards, breaking George Blanda's 1961 team record.

Late in the 1985 season, defensive coordinator Jerry Glanville was promoted to head coach. Glanville, known for his black attire and sharp wit, said his goal was to turn the Astrodome into a "House of Pain" for opponents—to make his team more aggressive and intimidating. "When I came here in '84, we had the nicest guys in the NFL," Glanville later said. "But they couldn't hit if you handed them sticks."

Glanville fortified his defense with swift cornerback Cris Dishman and linemen Ray Childress and William Fuller, while offensive lineman Bruce Matthews—who had joined the Oilers in 1983—helped stabilize the offense. Glanville built his offense around Moon, who quickly became a fan favorite akin to Earl Campbell. Fans flocked to the Astrodome, and the Oilers did not disappoint them. Houston finished 9–6 in 1987 and made the playoffs for the first of seven straight seasons.

The Eighth World Wonder

Originally called the Harris County Domed Stadium, the Houston Astrodome was built in 1965 to accommodate both baseball and football. The first domed stadium in professional sports, the facility boasted cushioned, theater-style seats, futuristic sky boxes, and a $2-million scoreboard. Major League Baseball's Houston Astros began using the stadium—dubbed the "Eighth Wonder of the World"—in 1965, and the Oilers moved in three years later. Semi-transparent panels on the roof originally allowed natural grass to grow inside the stadium, but baseball players often complained that they could not see fly balls against the cream-colored panels. So stadium officials painted the tiles darker colors, which killed the grass. To compensate, plastic grass called AstroTurf was installed to cover the stadium floor. The Astrodome seated roughly 50,000 fans, and it was known as a loud football stadium that made it difficult for opposing teams to hear play calls. After the 1996 season, the Oilers said goodbye to the Astrodome when they relocated to Tennessee, and the Astros departed from the dome in 2000. Today, the Astrodome stands largely vacant, hosting only an occasional business convention or softball game.

"CHEMGRASS" BECAME "ASTROTURF" AFTER THE PRODUCT WAS USED IN THE ASTRODOME

RUNNING BACK LORENZO WHITE BROKE AWAY FOR 1,226 YARDS IN 1992

Moving with McNair

Although Houston consistently made the postseason, the Oilers fell short of the Super Bowl every time. That inability to reach football's grandest stage led to a coaching change prior to the 1990 season, when Glanville was replaced by former NFL linebacker Jack Pardee. To take advantage of Moon's strong arm and scrambling ability, Coach Pardee installed the "run-and-shoot" offense, and Moon thrived in it. In a December 1990 road game against the Kansas City Chiefs, Moon passed for 527 yards, the second-highest total in NFL history at the time. In 1990 and 1991, Moon threw for nearly 4,700 yards each season. Catching most of his tosses were Jeffires and Hill. In 1991, Jeffires and Hill accumulated 190 receptions—at the time, the most ever by two teammates in one season.

Unfortunately, the Oilers' playoff woes continued. The most heartbreaking loss took place in the 1992 playoffs. The 10–6 Oilers traveled to Buffalo to face the Bills in the first round. Moon and the Oilers exploded from the gate, jumping to a 35–3 lead by early in

RAY CHILDRESS REPRESENTED DEFENSIVE ENDS IN THE PRO BOWL 5 TIMES

Bruce Matthews

GUARD, OFFENSIVE TACKLE, CENTER / OILERS/TITANS SEASONS: 1983–2001 /
HEIGHT: 6-FOOT-5 / WEIGHT: 305 POUNDS

The Oilers selected Bruce Matthews in the 1983 NFL Draft, and he served them well for the next 19 seasons. "He came off the ball with such quickness, got into his blocks, great finish," said Oilers offensive lineman Mike Munchak in describing the first time he saw Matthews in training camp. "His feet were all over the place. He was like a human weed whacker." By the second game of his rookie year, Matthews had secured a starting role on the offensive line as a guard. As time passed, he showed his versatility by playing every position on the line. Despite the physical toll of his job, the durable Matthews never missed a game because of injury. He was named to 14 consecutive Pro Bowls, tying Los Angeles Rams defensive tackle Merlin Olsen for the most in NFL history. By the time he retired, Matthews had competed in 296 games, which, at that time, was more than any non-kicker in league history. In fact, his career spanned so many years that his former college teammate, Jeff Fisher, became his NFL coach.

EDDIE GEORGE RUSHED FOR 10,009 YARDS WHILE WITH THE OILERS/TITANS

the third quarter. But the Bills fought back, combining quick-strike touchdown passes with daring onside kicks. In the greatest comeback in NFL playoff history, the Bills tied the game at 38–38, forcing overtime. Minutes later, Buffalo booted a field goal to seal Houston's collapse.

To the dismay of Houston fans, the Oilers traded Moon to the Minnesota Vikings in 1994, and in the midst of the team's first losing season in eight years, Coach Pardee was fired. Defensive coordinator Jeff Fisher was promoted to head coach, and he quickly began rebuilding the roster. Under Fisher's watch, Houston drafted quarterback Steve "Air" McNair in 1995 and running back Eddie George the following year. Together, the duo would become the heart of the team's offense. McNair was tough and versatile, equally adept at launching long bombs or scrambling for a first down. George, who would earn NFL Offensive Rookie of the Year honors in 1996, was a bruising runner who would never miss a start because of injury in his career with the club.

In addition to these roster changes, the Oilers made a geographic change as well. In 1995, Adams, who had long wanted a new stadium for his team but received little support for it in Houston, announced his intention to move the Oilers to Tennessee in 1997. While a new stadium was under construction in Nashville, the Oilers played in the Liberty Bowl in Memphis for a year and then moved to Vanderbilt Stadium in Nashville for the next season. During both of these transitional years, the

Oilers went a mediocre 8–8. Meanwhile, Tennessee fans clamored for a new team name that better reflected the franchise's new home. Adams listened, and in 1999, the former Oilers took the field as the Tennessee Titans.

In addition to their new name, logo, and uniforms, the Titans had a new star: defensive end Jevon Kearse, the team's top pick in the 1999 NFL Draft. Standing 6-foot-4 and weighing 265 pounds, Kearse had such rare speed and agility that he was nicknamed "The Freak." Kearse lived up to expectations, setting an NFL rookie record with 14.5 quarterback sacks in 1999. McNair, meanwhile, led a powerful offense. George rushed for 1,304 yards in 1999, and safety Blaine Bishop and cornerback Samari Rolle headed up a tough defense. The Titans finished the regular season 13–3, going unbeaten at their new home stadium,

JEVON KEARSE WAS A POWERFULLY STEALTHY TACKLER FOR THE TITANS

The Music City Miracle

The "Music City Miracle" unfolded during an opening-round playoff game between the Titans and the Buffalo Bills in January 2000. The Bills kicked a field goal with 16 seconds left, moving ahead 16–15 and needing only to keep the Titans from scoring. Titans running back Lorenzo Neal received the kick and handed it off to tight end Frank Wycheck. Wycheck then drifted right before stopping and passing the ball across the field to wide receiver Kevin Dyson, who then ran 75 yards along the sideline to score the game-winning touchdown as the Titans' Adelphia Coliseum crowd went crazy. The play, called "Home Run Throwback," was the brainchild of Titans special-teams coach Alan Lowry. Incredibly, Dyson had replaced an injured teammate for the kick return. Titans coach Jeff Fisher was still explaining the trick play as Dyson ran onto the field. "It was like being a little kid again, drawing something up in the dirt and then going out and doing it," Wycheck said. Bills coach Wade Phillips challenged the legality of the lateral pass, but replays showed the pass was indeed sideways, and the "miracle" was upheld.

KEVIN DYSON'S SIDELINE RUN CAUGHT THE ATTENTION OF EVERYONE

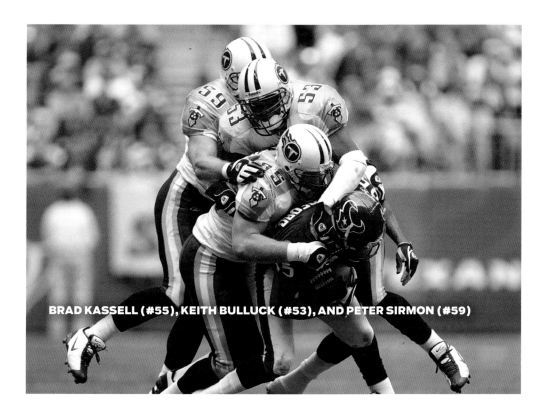

BRAD KASSELL (#55), KEITH BULLUCK (#53), AND PETER SIRMON (#59)

Adelphia Coliseum. Tennessee continued to roll through the playoffs. The Titans won their first playoff game against the Bills with an unbelievable kickoff return in the final seconds of the game.

Tennessee followed the "Music City Miracle" by fighting past the Indianapolis Colts and the Jacksonville Jaguars to reach the Super Bowl for the first time in franchise history. In a matchup against the high-scoring St. Louis Rams, the Titans came back from a 16–0 deficit to tie the game. The Rams took a 23–16 lead with 1 minute and 54 seconds left on the clock, and McNair drove the Titans down the field. Sadly, they were stopped just short of a chance at victory when Tennessee receiver Kevin Dyson was pulled down one yard shy of the end zone as time expired.

In the four seasons after their Super Bowl appearance, the Titans remained one of the elite teams of the NFL, though they could not make it back to the big game. Led by McNair's strong arm and tough-as-nails leadership, as well as George's relentless rushing, Tennessee made the playoffs in 2000, 2002, and 2003, and posted records of 13–3, 11–5, and 12–4 during those years.

The 2003 season was particularly rewarding for McNair. In one game against the new Houston Texans team, McNair played with a cracked bone spur in one leg and a sore calf in the other, but he led the Titans down the field in the final minutes of the game and connected with receiver Drew Bennett for the winning score. In the playoffs, the Titans beat the Baltimore Ravens 20–17 before losing to the Patriots in a frigid matchup. After the season, McNair was named the NFL's co-Most Valuable Player (MVP), along with Colts quarterback Peyton Manning.

BO SCAIFE FIRST CAUGHT VINCE YOUNG PASSES AT THE UNIVERSITY OF TEXAS

Titanic Effort

That season signaled the end of an era in Tennessee. After the 2003 season, the Titans went into rebuilding mode and began clearing out veterans to make way for younger players. The Titans released George in 2004; two seasons later, they traded McNair to the Ravens after selecting quarterback Vince Young with the third overall pick in the 2006 NFL Draft. "We're a scrappy, young team, definitely one of the future teams in the NFL," Titans linebacker Keith Bulluck said.

At 6-foot-5 and fast on his feet, Young was a bigger version of McNair, and he quickly became Tennessee's starter in his first season. The rookie wasted no time in showing a knack for leading his team to comeback victories. In a November 2006 game against the New York Giants, the Titans trailed 21–0 after three quarters. Young then orchestrated the biggest fourth-quarter rally in the club's history. After hitting tight end Bo Scaife on a four-yard touchdown pass, Young ran the ball himself for a score and then tossed another touchdown—this time to Brandon Jones—with 23 seconds left on the clock.

VINCE YOUNG'S ARM POWERED THE TITANS' OFFENSE FOR 5 SEASONS

Jeff Fisher

COACH / OILERS/TITANS SEASONS: 1994–2010

In the early 1980s, Jeff Fisher played as a defensive back and kick returner for the Chicago Bears. After an ankle injury ended his NFL playing career in 1985, he turned to coaching. By 1988, he was the Philadelphia Eagles' defensive coordinator, the youngest in the NFL. He joined the Houston Oilers as defensive coordinator in 1994 and earned the head coaching job later that year. His defensive background shaped his coaching philosophy. With the Titans, Fisher built solid rushing defenses and strong running games, encouraging his players to remain poised when faced with adversity. He also showed an ability to take the team from a disappointing start to a promising finish, leading the 1–4 Titans to an 11–5 finish in 2002. By 2005, he owned the team record for wins by a head coach, and by 2008, he had coached more than 200 regular-season games for the franchise. Despite his lengthy tenure, Fisher kept his outlook fresh each season. "It's like every year is my first year," he said in 2007. "I really look forward to coming to work."

The Titans' defense then made an interception, and with six seconds remaining in regulation, kicker Rob Bironas nailed a 49-yard, game-winning field goal to stun the Giants. At season's end, Young was named to the Pro Bowl, making him the first rookie quarterback since Miami Dolphins great Dan Marino (in 1983) to receive such an honor.

In 2007, big defensive tackle Albert Haynesworth emerged as the Titans' newest defensive standout. And with young running back LenDale White pounding out 1,110 yards on the ground, the Titans fought their way to a 10–6 record, good enough for a playoff spot. Although they promptly lost to the San Diego Chargers, 17–6, the off-season addition of rookie running back Chris Johnson made them even stronger.

ALBERT HAYNESWORTH SOMETIMES TOOK HIS AGGRESSIVE PLAY TOO FAR

KEITH BULLUCK'S DECADE IN TENNESSEE GAVE HIM INSIGHT INTO TEAMMATES

The Titans were one of the biggest stories in the NFL in 2008. They started the season 10–0 behind veteran quarterback Kerry Collins (who was named the starter after Young was injured) and finished the year 13–3 to secure a first-round playoff bye and home-field advantage in the postseason. Unfortunately, despite outplaying Baltimore in a second-round matchup, the Titans turned the ball over three times, losing 13–10 and ending an otherwise superb season on a sour note.

The following season started, unfortunately, with sadness. Over the summer, longtime Titans quarterback Steve McNair was shot and killed by a jealous girlfriend. As fans and former teammates tried to make sense of the tragedy, the Titans decided to honor his 11-year career with the team by placing decals featuring McNair's number 9 on every player's helmet for the duration of the 2009 season. "It's very much well-deserved for the person Mac was in this community, who he was on this team, what he meant to this organization and the players that he's influenced big and small over the years," Bulluck said.

The team seemed to be in mourning as it started the season 0–6 and endured its most embarrassing loss ever, a 59–0 drubbing at the hands of the Patriots. But after a much-needed bye week, the Titans won their next five games and ended the season with a solid 8–8 record. Along the way, Johnson rushed for 2,006 yards, becoming only the 6th player in NFL history to attain at least 2,000 yards in a season.

Bironas Gets His Kicks

When Titans kicker Rob Bironas kicked 35 field goals in 2007, he not only led the league in field goals, but he also led his team in scoring. With 133 points on the season, Bironas brought consistency to every game. Before his arrival in Tennessee, he had spent time in training camp with the Green Bay Packers, Tampa Bay Buccaneers, and Pittsburgh Steelers while also playing Arena League Football. After he found a home with the Titans in 2005, his long, accurate last-second field goals determined the game for the Titans on more than one occasion. While usual field-goal range is about 54 yards, Bironas made history in December 2006, when his game-winning field goal against the Indianapolis Colts soared 60 yards to pass through the goalposts. Bironas became only the sixth kicker in NFL history to successfully score a field goal from 60 yards or farther. He revisited the league history books in 2007, when he connected on a record eight field goals in a Titans win over the Houston Texans. "We'd rather have touchdowns," said Titans running back Chris Brown, "but we know when he goes out, it's good."

ROB BIRONAS ALSO GOT A KICK OUT OF HELPING NASHVILLE YOUTH EXPERIENCE MUSIC

WILL WITHERSPOON HAD A TOTAL OF 62 BIG HITS IN 2010, PLUS 29 TACKLE ASSISTS

Although that effort wasn't good enough to get Tennessee back to the playoffs, it did lift the team's sagging spirits and served as a fitting tribute to the tenacious quarterback who had been on players' minds all season.

The 2010 season got off to a much better start, thanks in part to the efforts of newly signed linebacker Will Witherspoon and busy wide receiver Kenny Britt, who caught a career-high seven receptions with three touchdowns in a 37–19 win over the Philadelphia Eagles. But it didn't end quite as well: the Titans lost eight of the final nine games of the season to finish with a disappointing 6–10 record. Afterward, longtime coach Jeff Fisher was fired, and former Oilers player Mike Munchak was brought in as the new head coach.

Veteran quarterback Matt Hasselbeck joined the Titans for the 2011 season and, with durable running back Chris Johnson, helped the team put together a winning record and come close to qualifying for a

Steve McNair

QUARTERBACK / OILERS/TITANS SEASONS: 1995–2005 / HEIGHT: 6-FOOT-2 / WEIGHT: 235 POUNDS

Nicknamed "Air" McNair in college because of his ability to make big plays with his rifle of an arm, Steve McNair spent the majority of his first two seasons with the Oilers on the bench, learning plays and observing the team's offense. When he took the reins in 1997, McNair showed tremendous running skill and the ability to stay cool under pressure. He scrambled for 674 rushing yards that season, then went to work perfecting his passing accuracy. McNair led his team to the Super Bowl following the 1999 season, and he won league co-MVP honors in 2003. Despite the long list of injuries that plagued him, McNair displayed an unusual tolerance for pain. During 2002, his injuries caused him to miss most practices. Yet he started every game that season and amassed 3,387 passing yards. McNair was so respected in Nashville that, upon his tragic death in 2009, thousands came to LP Field to mourn his passing. "If ever there was a better connection between a city and a player, I haven't seen it," sportswriter Clay Travis wrote. "McNair and Nashville were a perfect pair."

CHRIS JOHNSON'S CONSISTENTLY HIGH YARDAGE WAS AN ASSET TO THE TITANS

JAKE LOCKER DISPLAYED HIS ATHLETICISM AND LEADERSHIP SKILLS IN 2012

CORNERBACK JASON McCOURTY CELEBRATED 4 INTERCEPTIONS IN 2012

spot in the playoffs. With Hasselbeck mentoring young quarterback Jake Locker, Tennessee's first-round pick in the 2011 NFL Draft, the team looked forward to building an offense that would help it return to postseason play for the first time in four seasons. Although the Titans finished second in the AFC South Division, the postseason eluded them yet again.

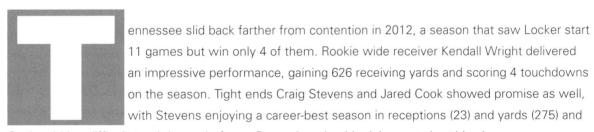

Tennessee slid back farther from contention in 2012, a season that saw Locker start 11 games but win only 4 of them. Rookie wide receiver Kendall Wright delivered an impressive performance, gaining 626 receiving yards and scoring 4 touchdowns on the season. Tight ends Craig Stevens and Jared Cook showed promise as well, with Stevens enjoying a career-best season in receptions (23) and yards (275) and Cook nabbing difficult touchdowns before a December shoulder injury cut short his play.

Although a Super Bowl win was not in the cards for the Oilers and hasn't been part of the Titans' experience yet, either, a winning tradition has followed this franchise throughout its history. Tennessee fans are confident that it won't be long before their Titans bring the Lombardi Trophy home to Nashville, giving their proud city yet another claim to fame.

INDEX